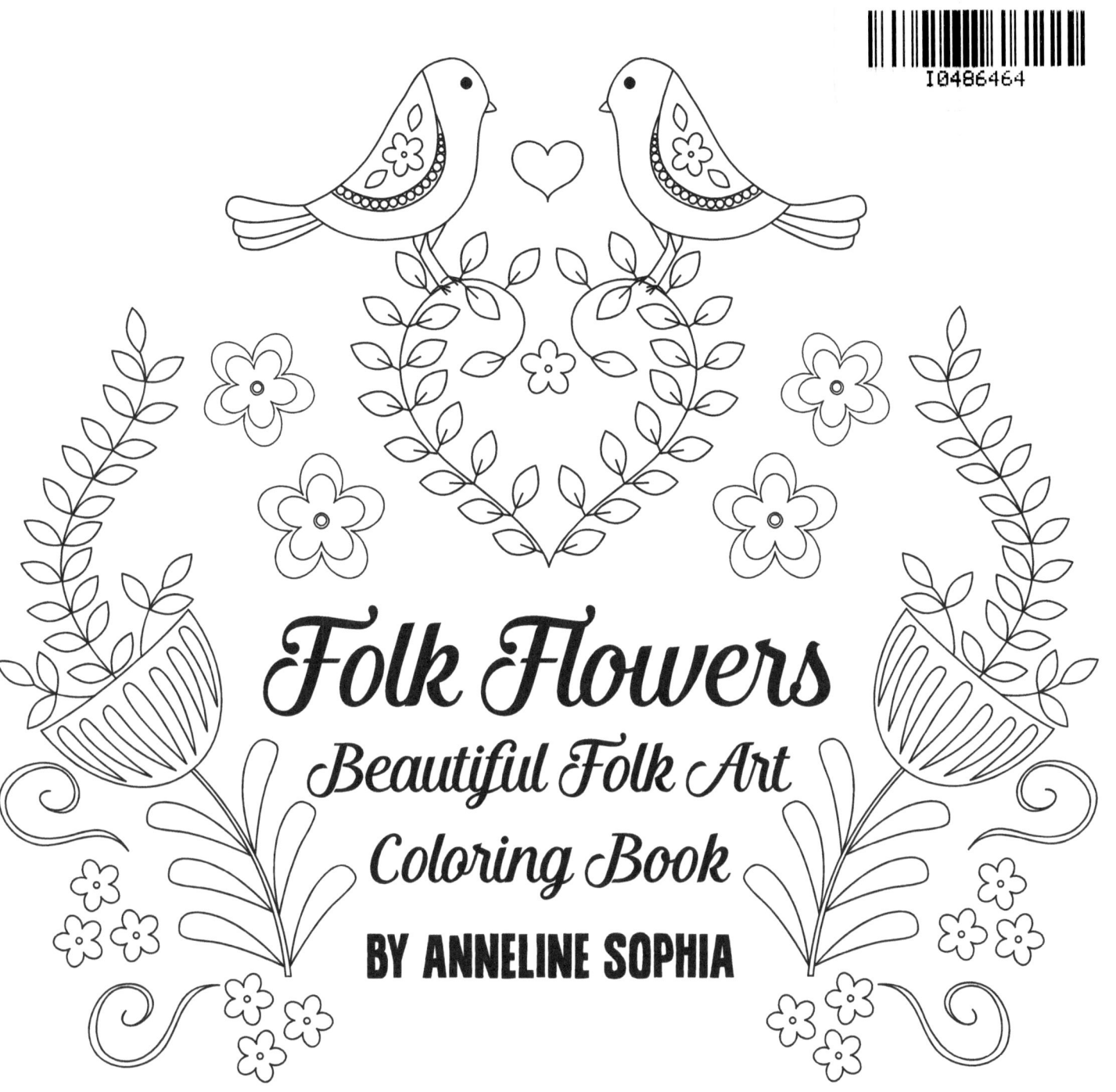

Folk Flowers
Beautiful Folk Art Coloring Book
BY ANNELINE SOPHIA

Folk Flowers – Beautiful Folk Art Coloring Book

©2015 Anneline Sophia

www.annelinesophiadesigns.com

For the beautiful women in my life. My mom for instilling in me a love of flowers.
My sister, Gerda, for encouraging me and believing in me.
For my beautiful daughter, Isla, for being Mama's biggest fan and for all the giggles
and flower adventures on our daily walks.
You are all a blessing and an inspiration to me!

With special thanks to my husband, Roger, my rock and support through all
my endeavours.

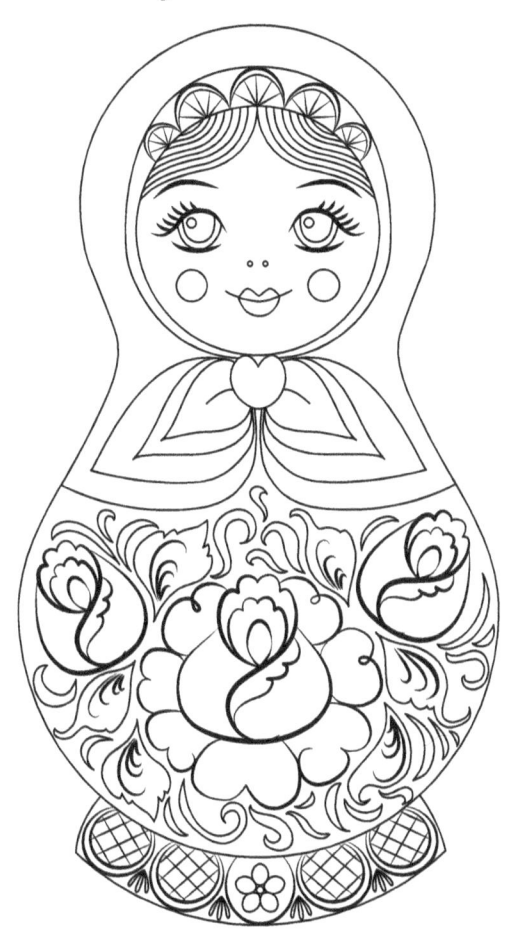

Due to the nature of the theme of this book, some of the motifs are detailed
and small to reflect the decorative elements of folk art which are sometimes
delicate emrboidery or detailed brush strokes. The best media to use is colored
pencils, gel pens and fine tip markers. Place a blank sheet of paper behind
the page you are coloring to prevent bleed through.

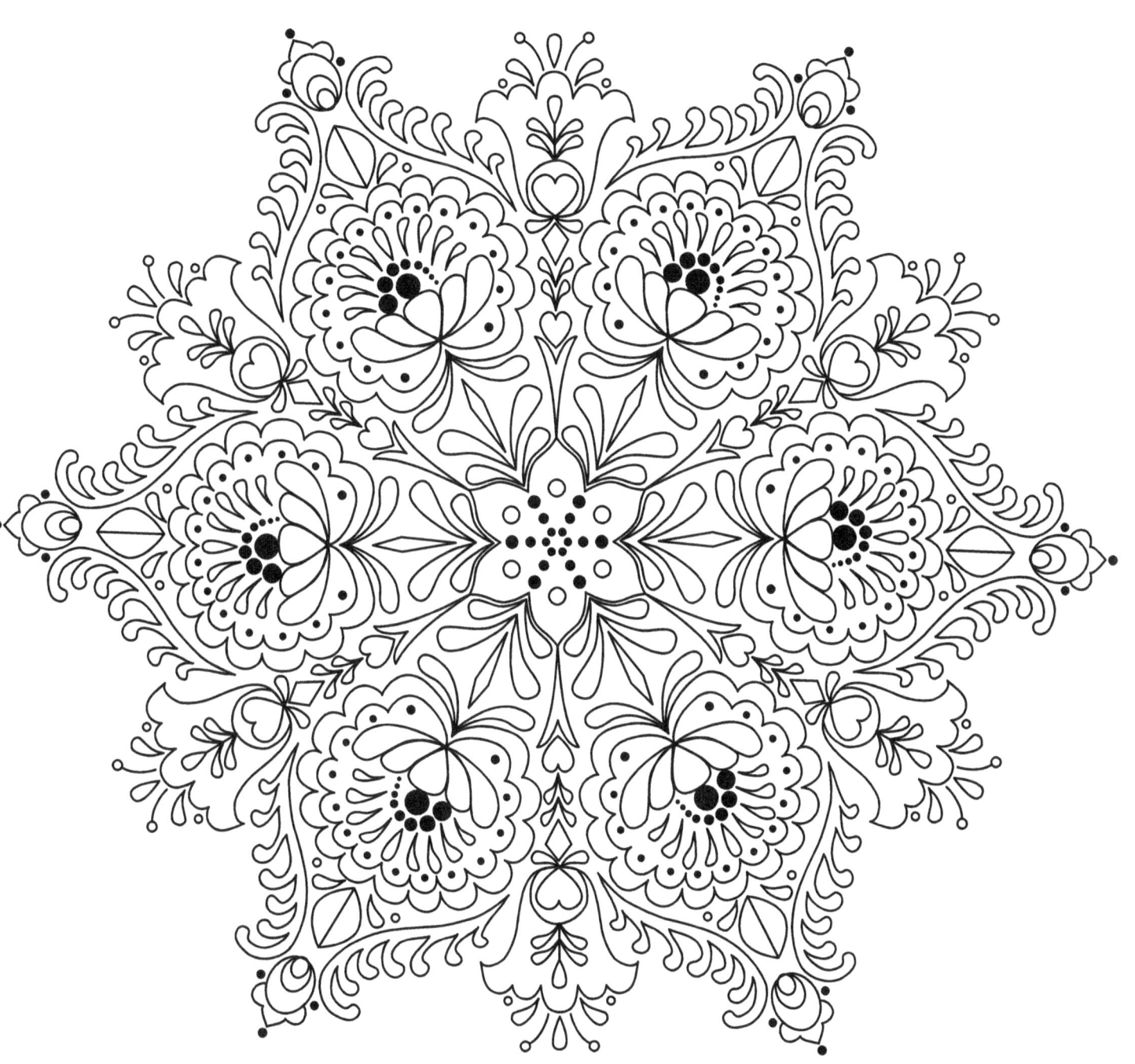

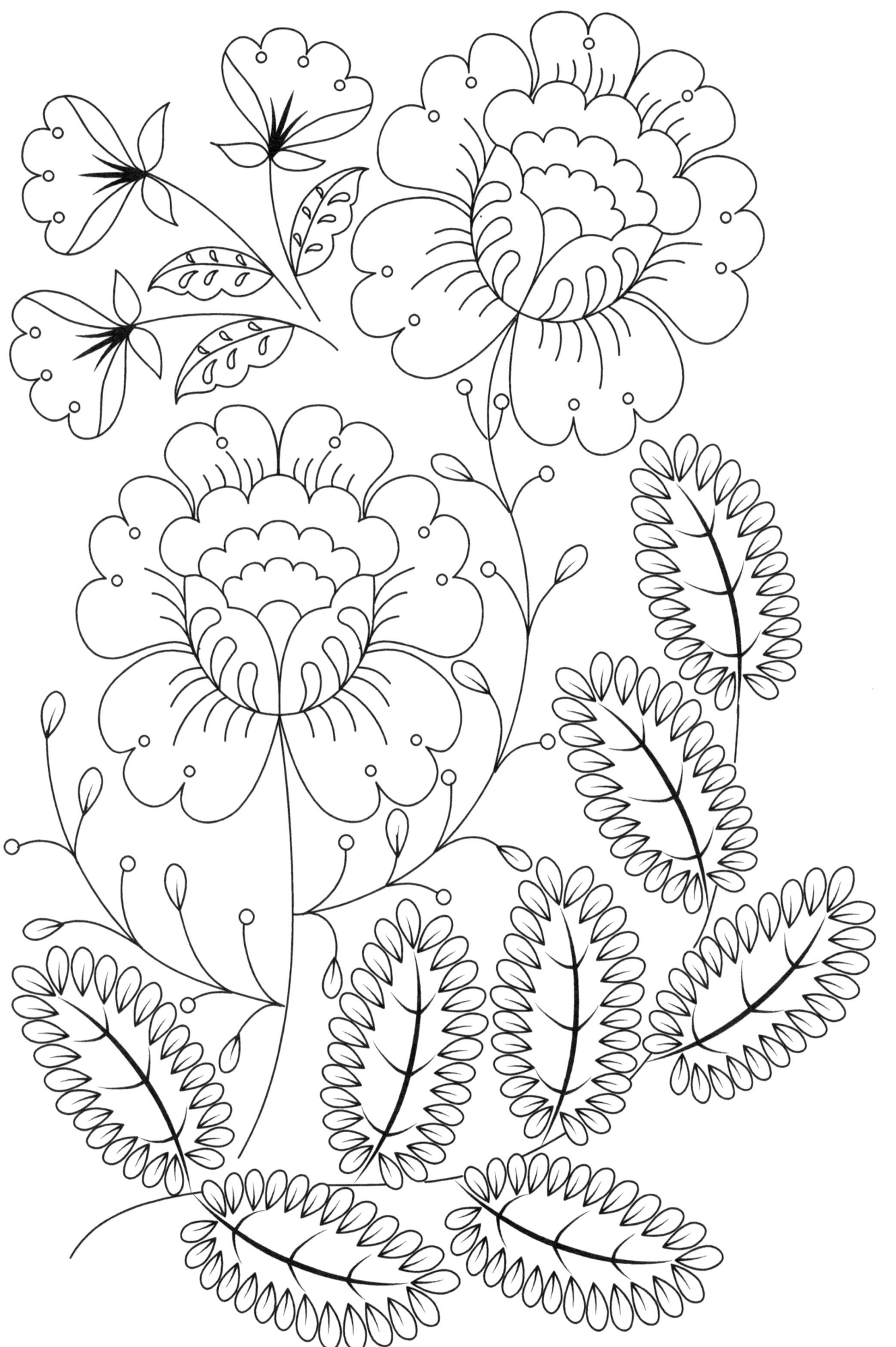

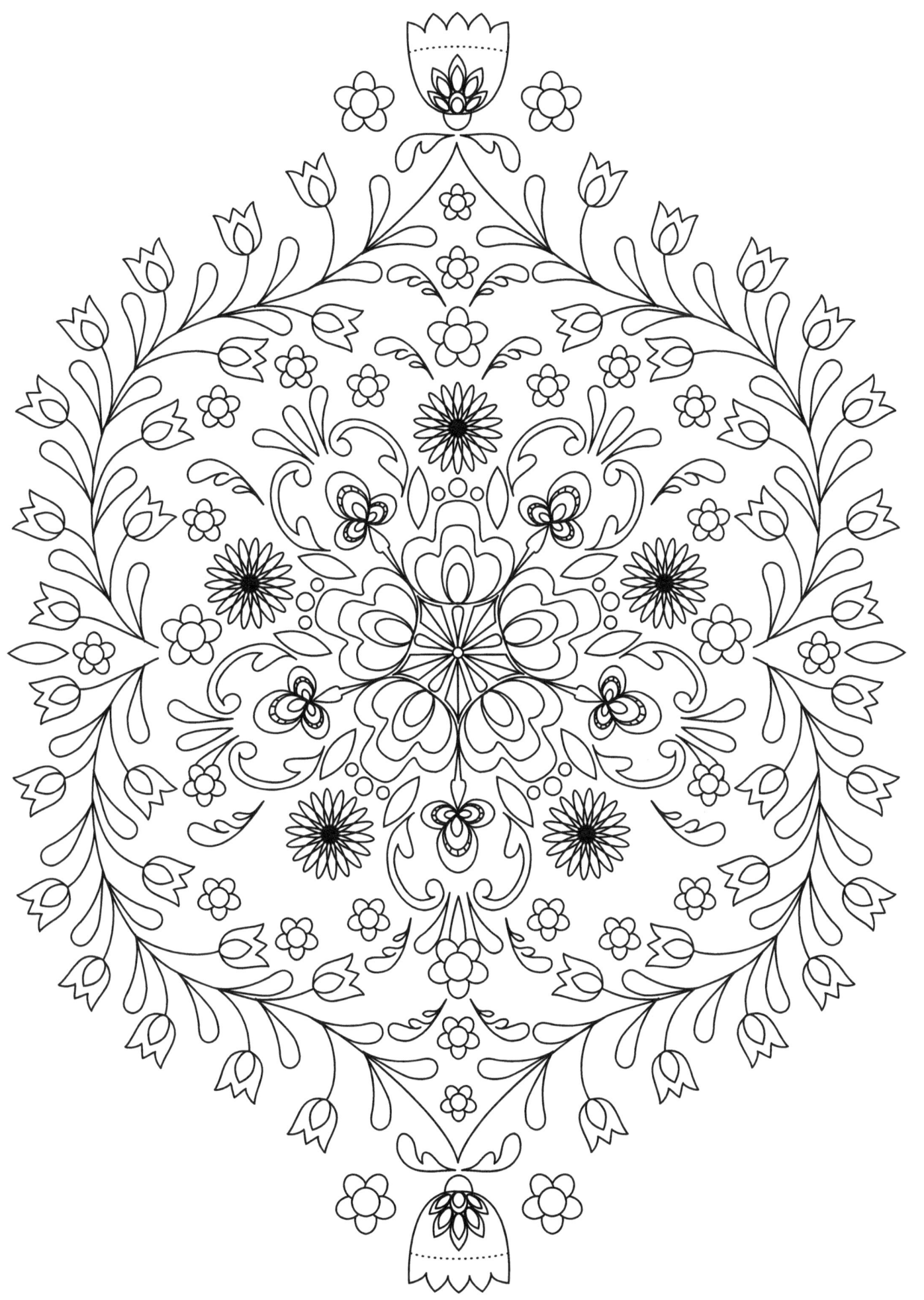

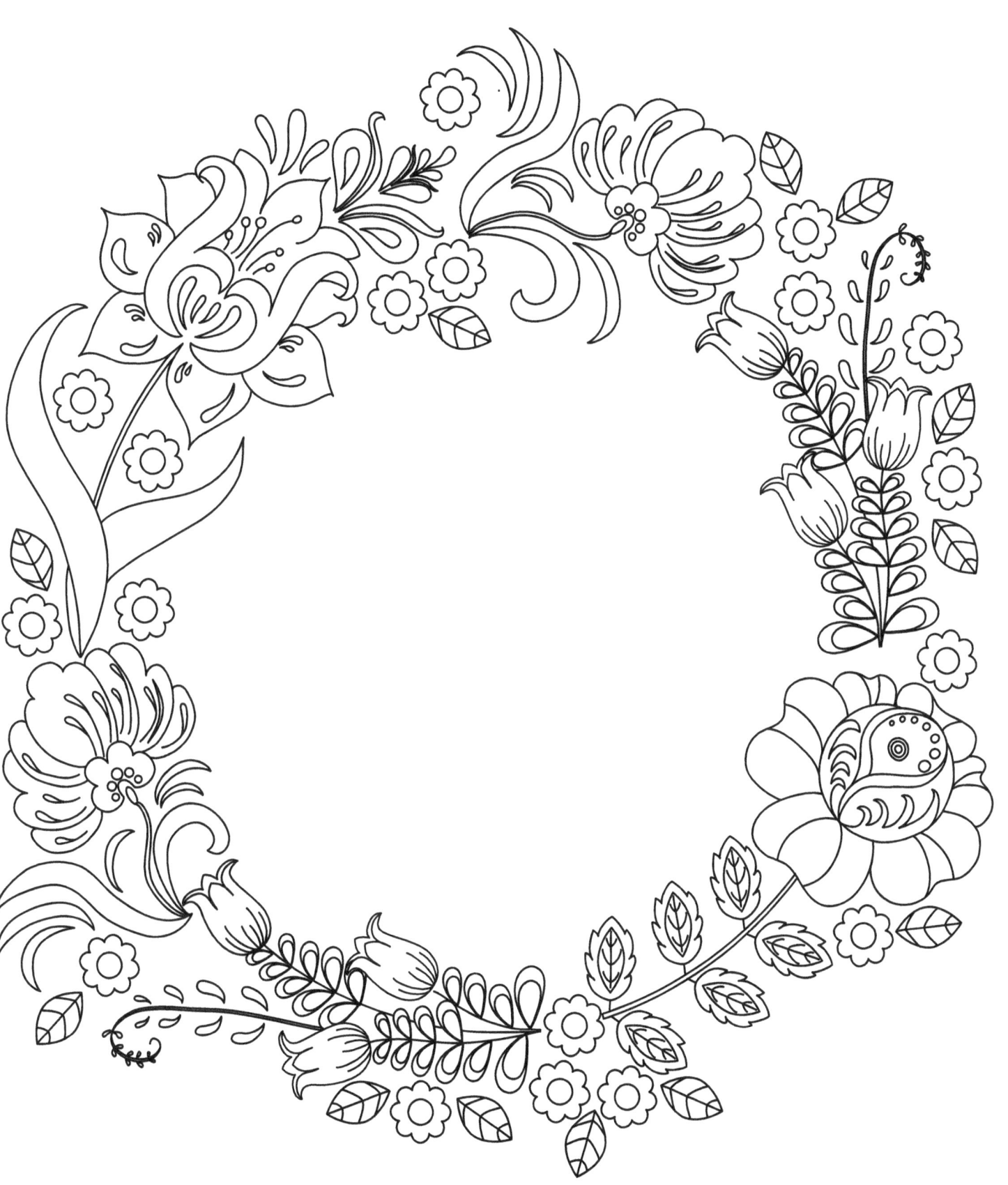

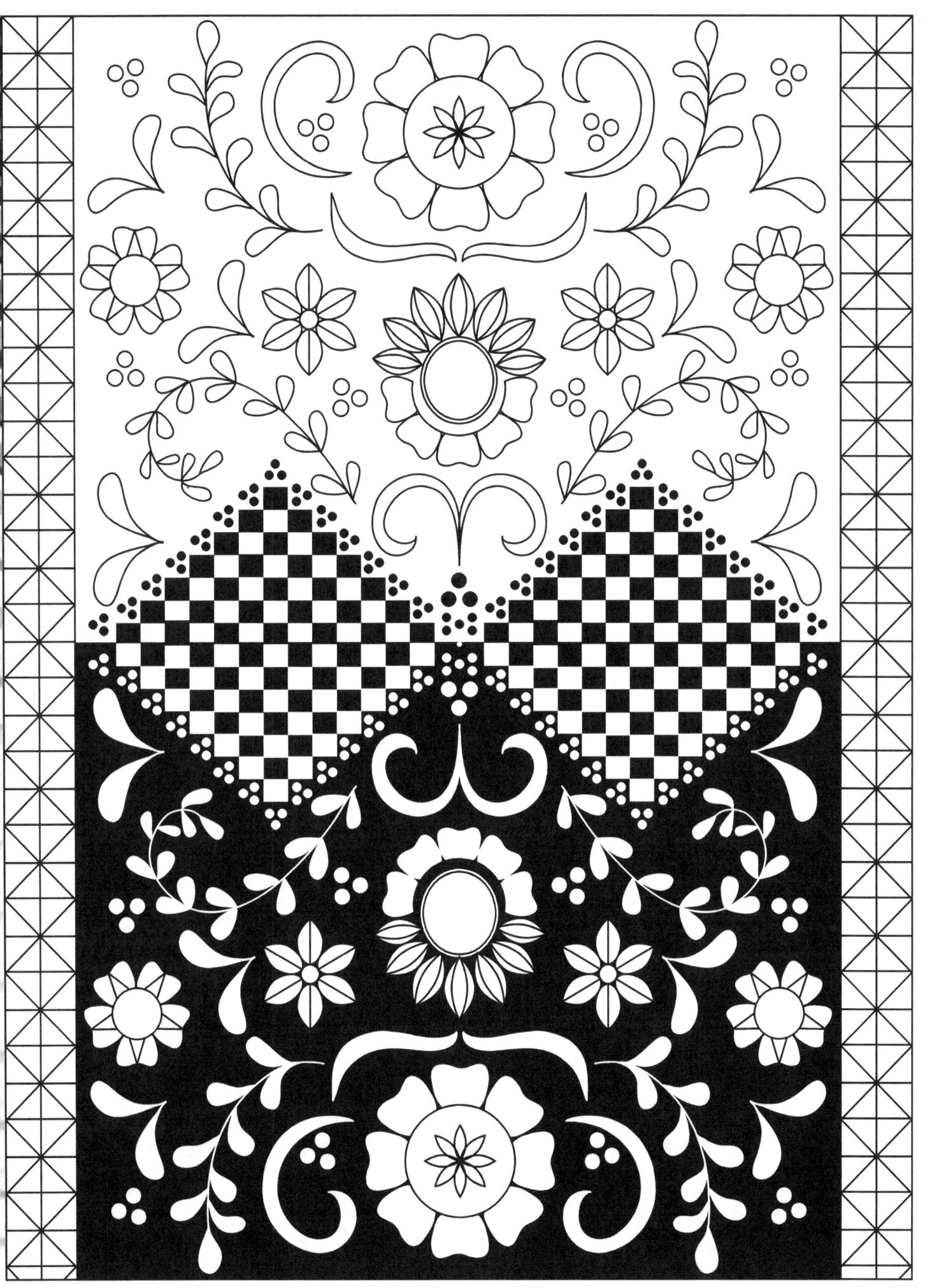

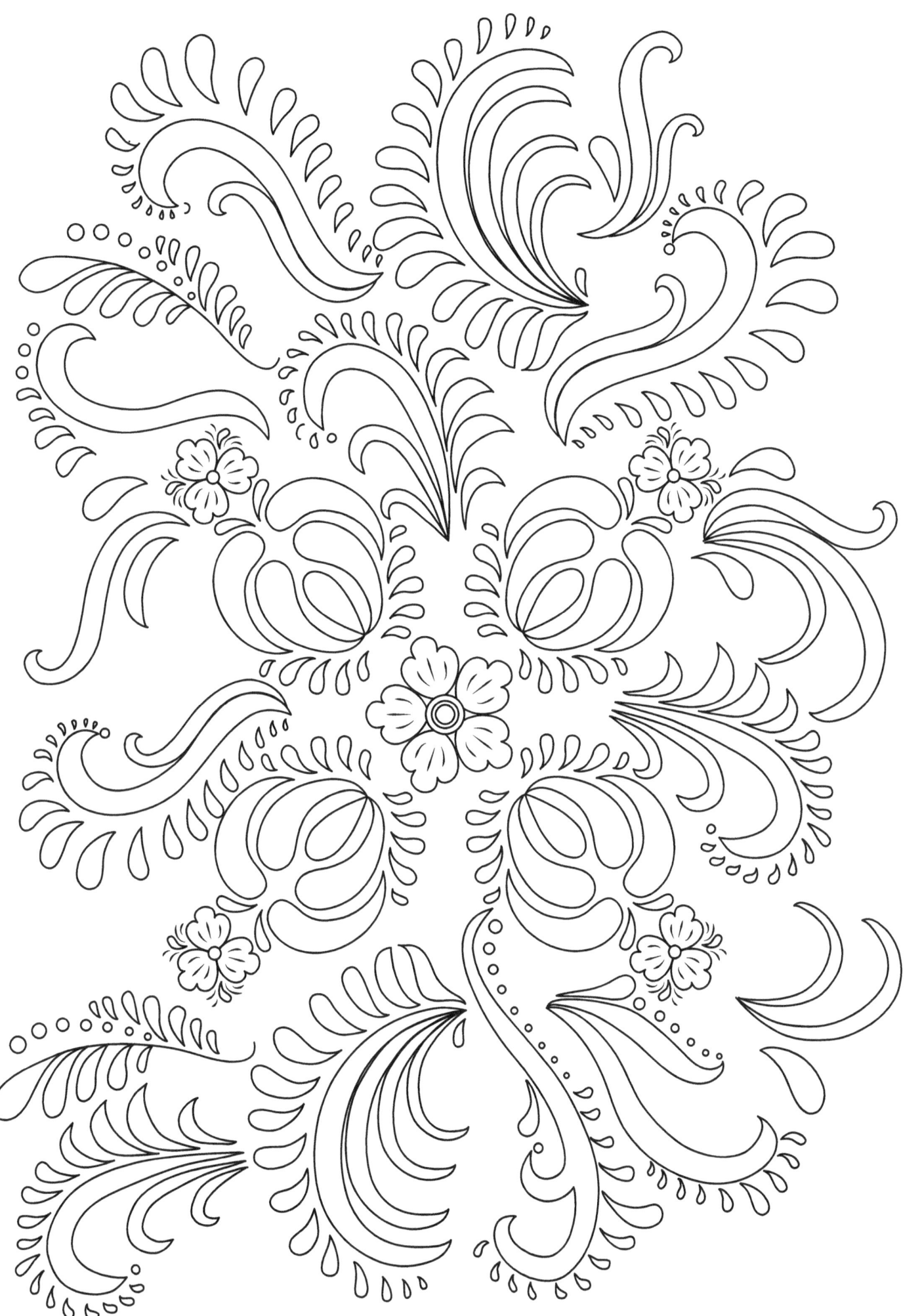

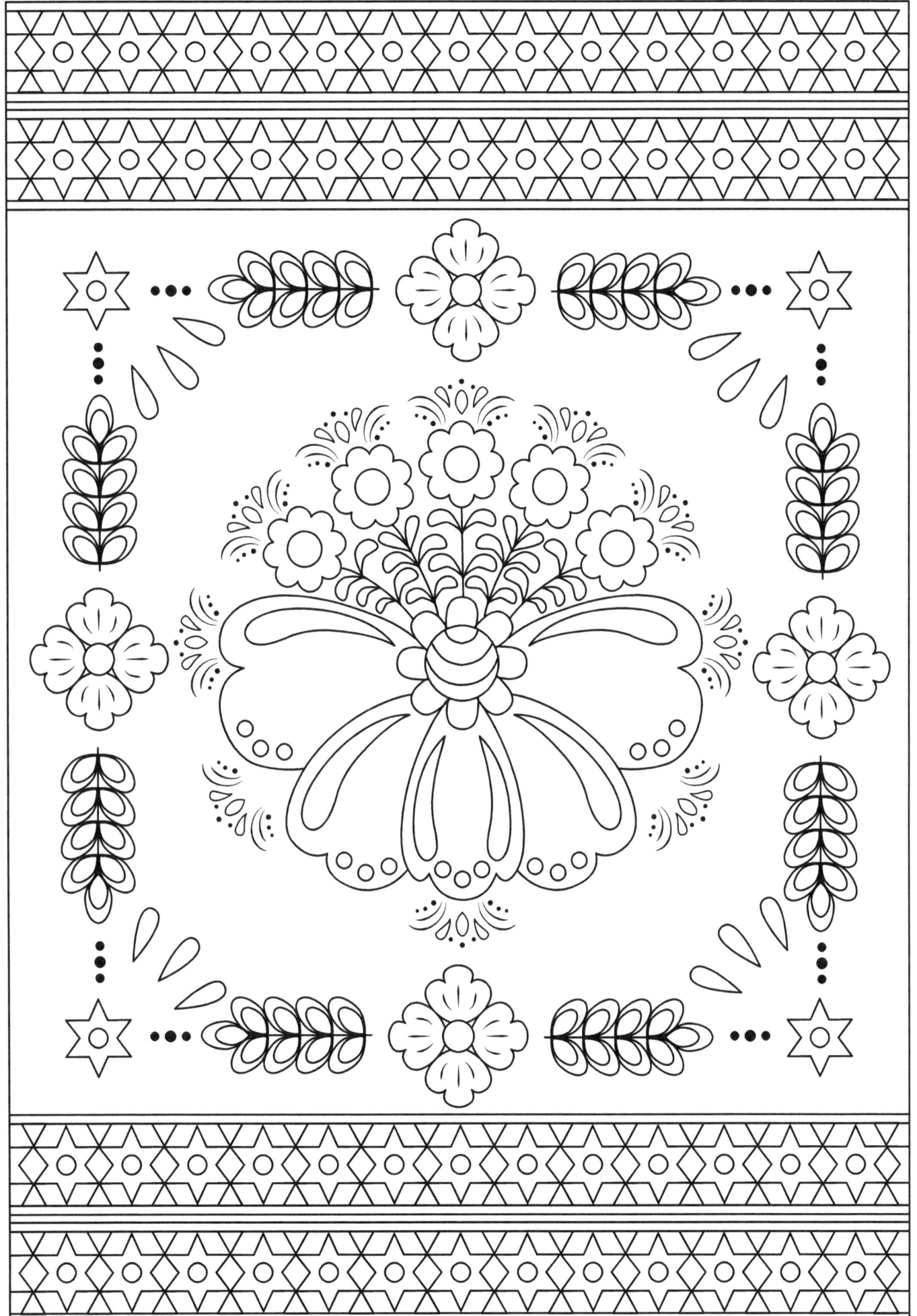

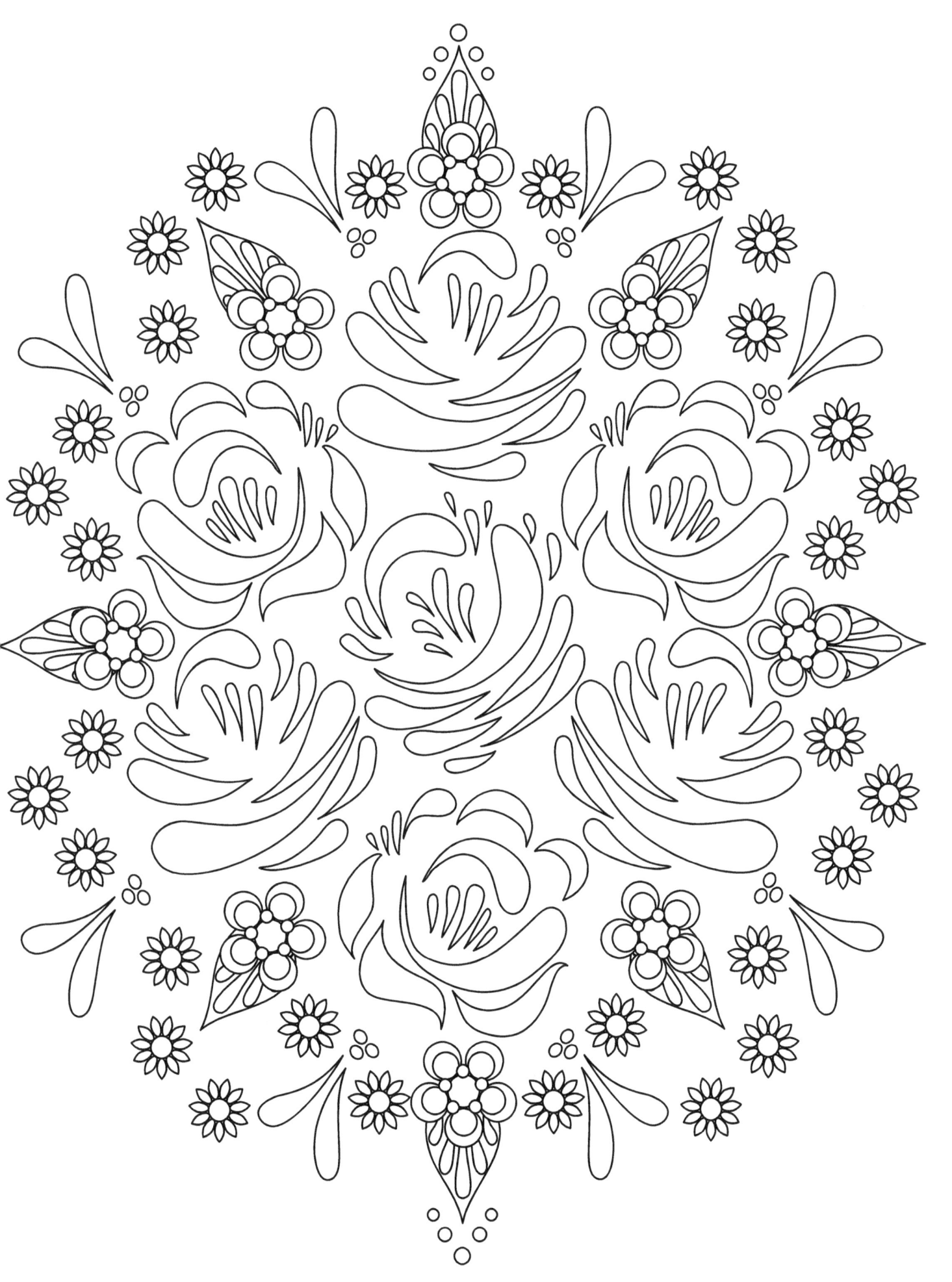

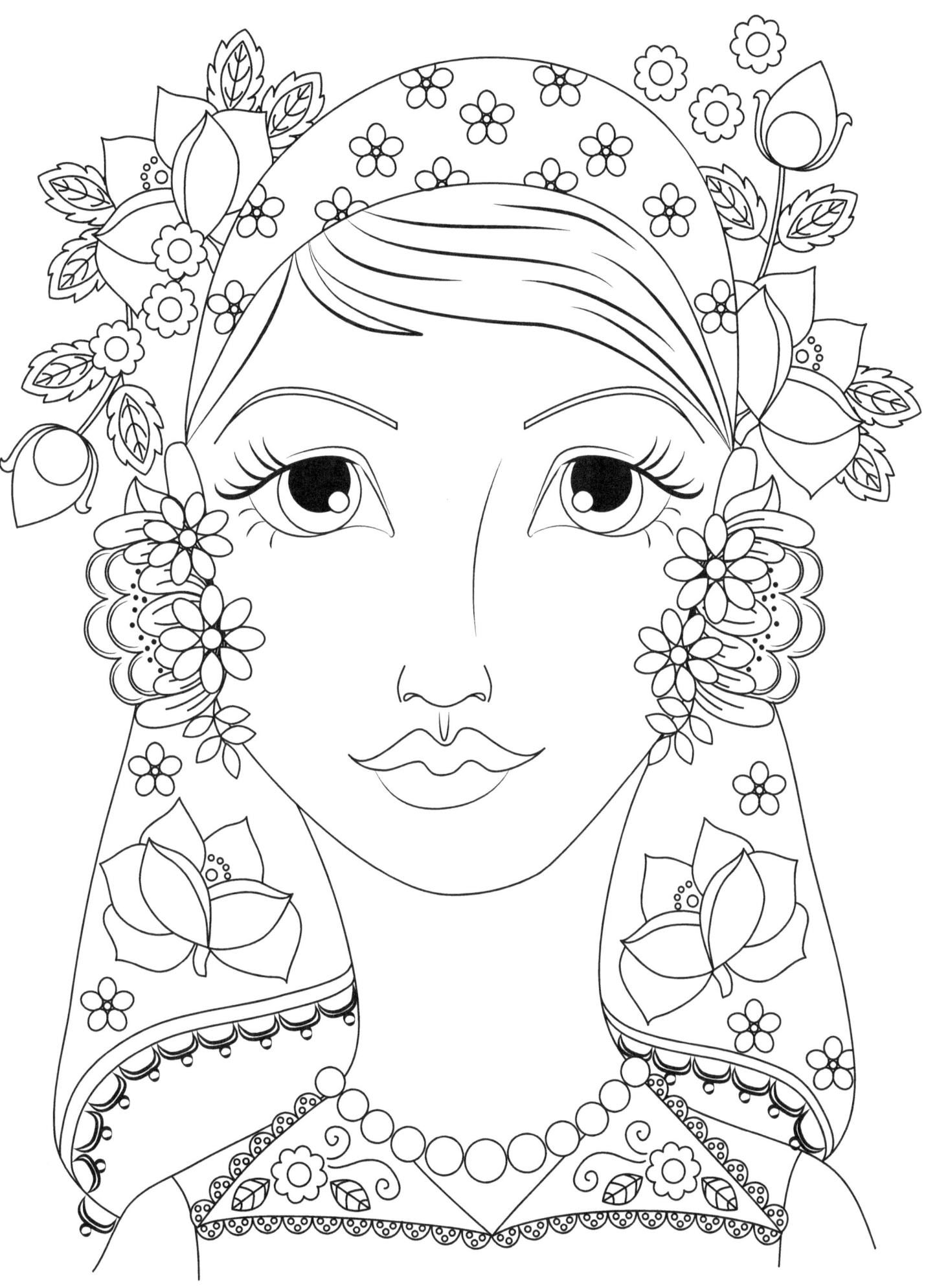

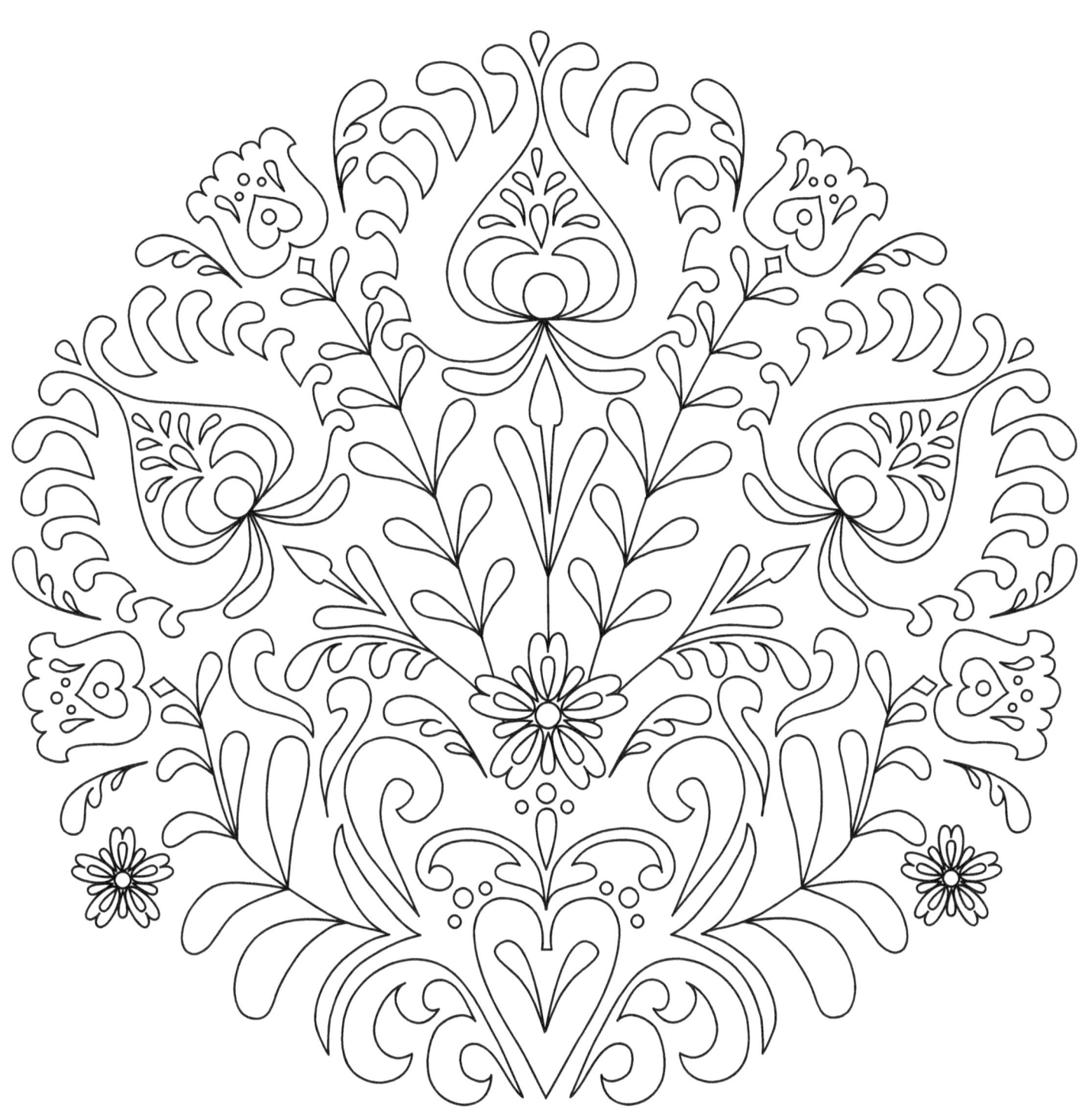

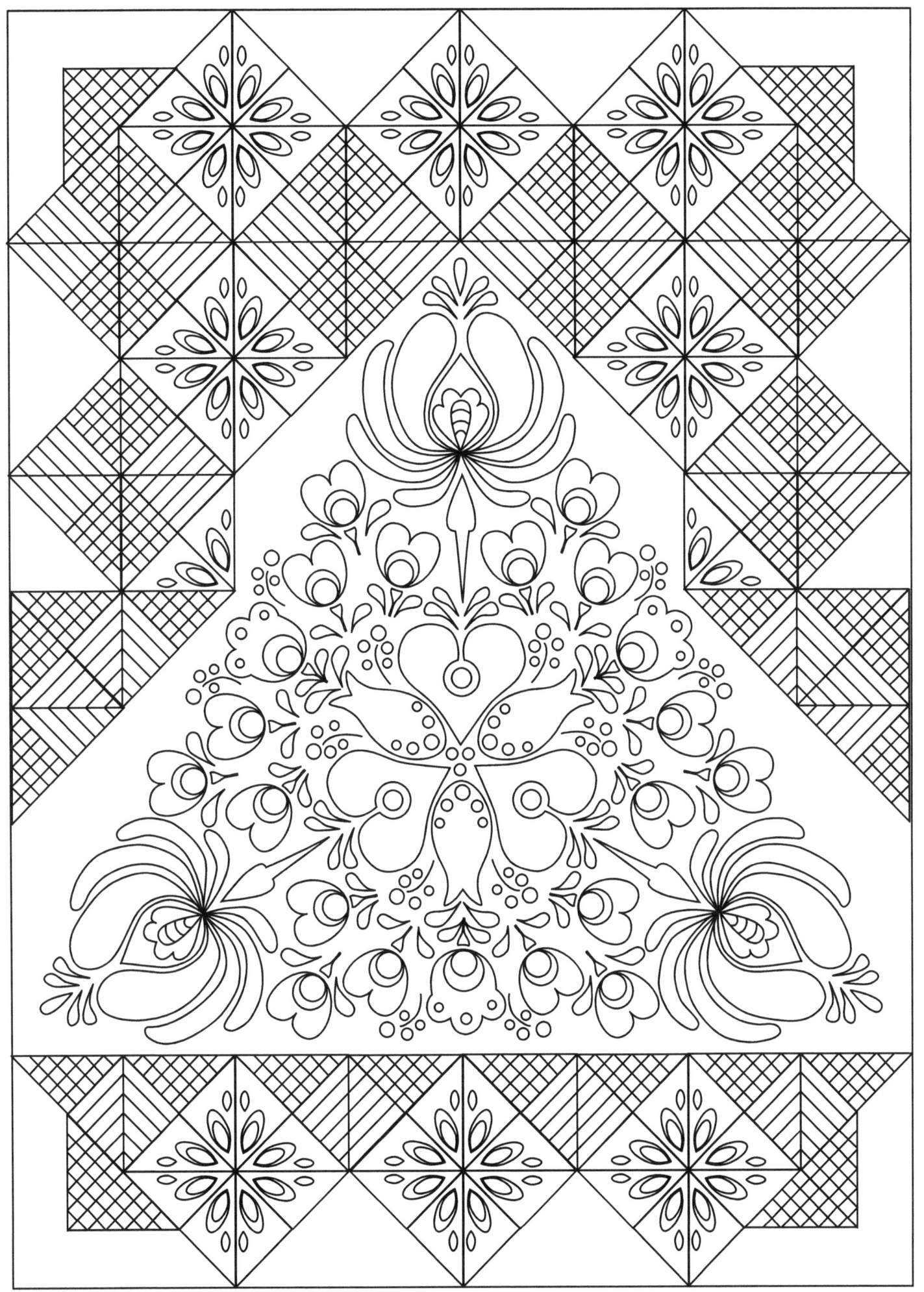

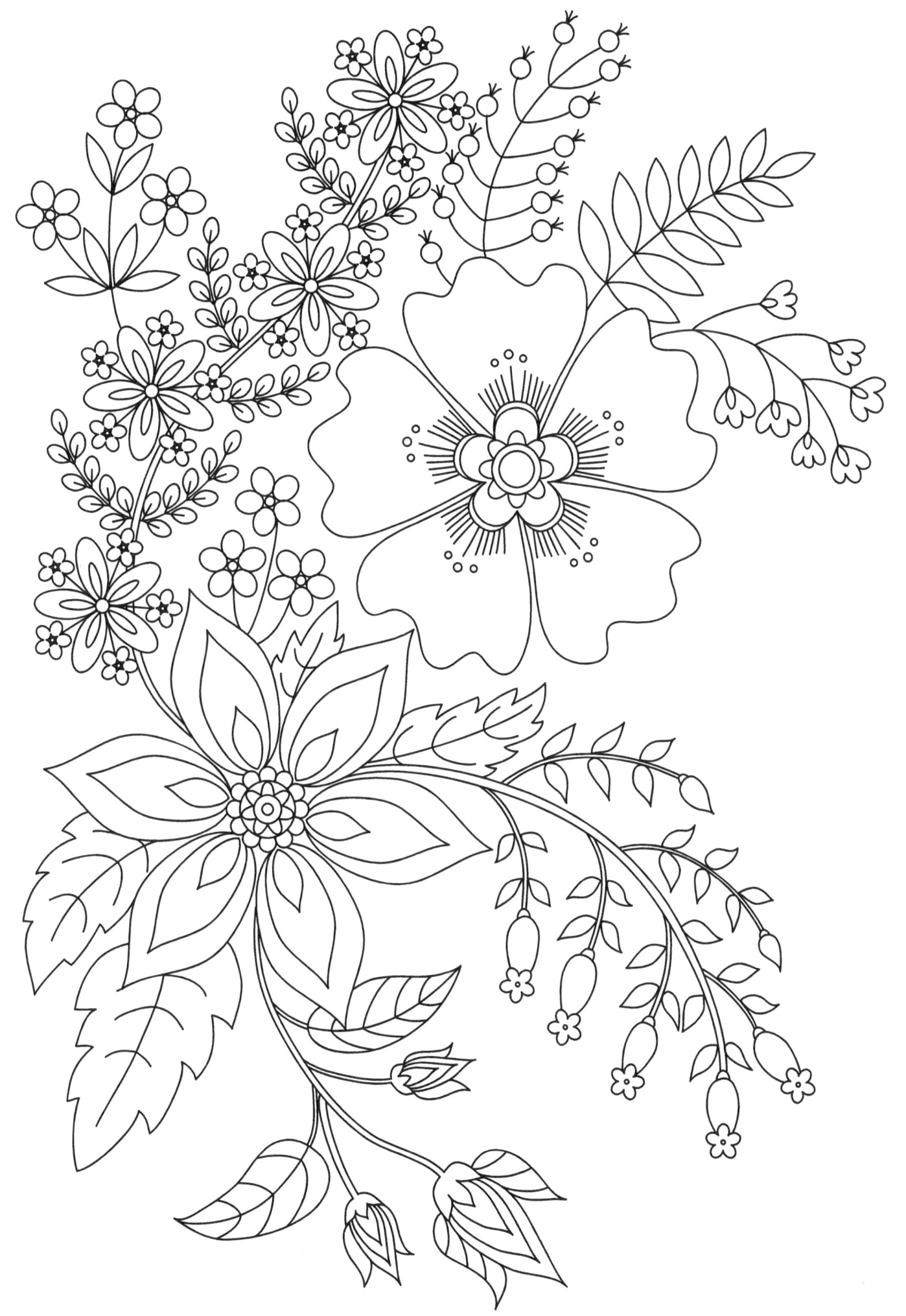

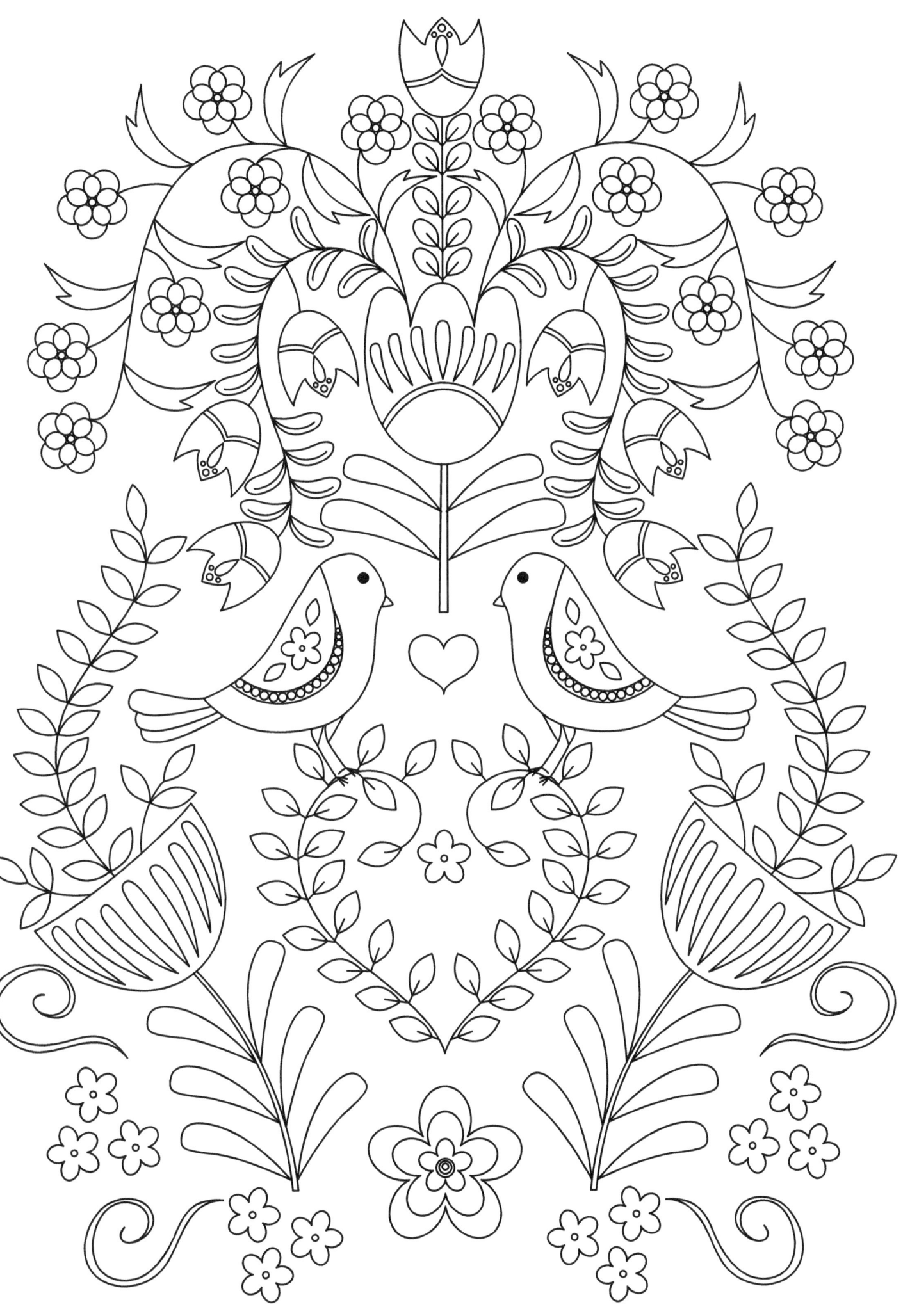

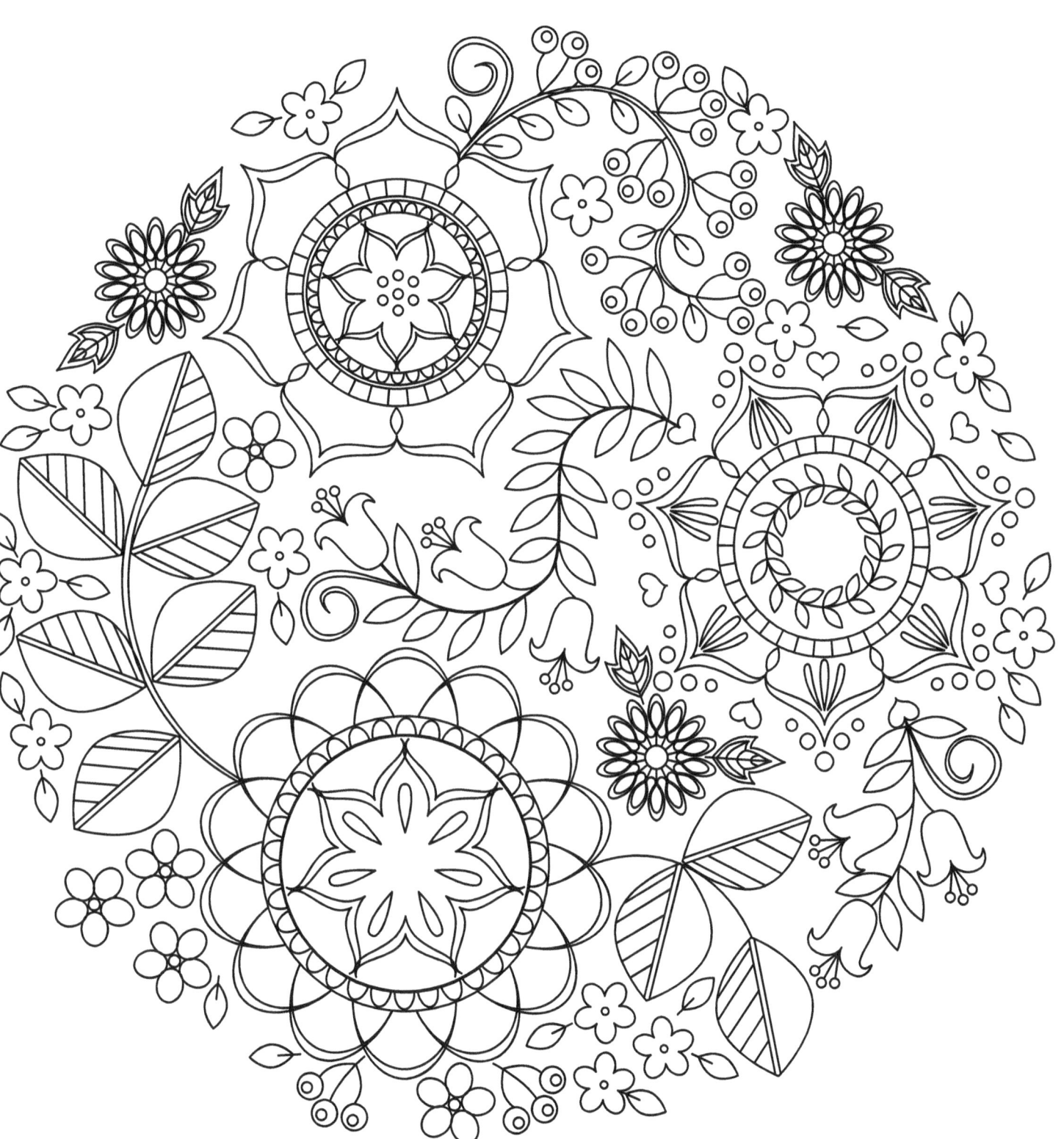

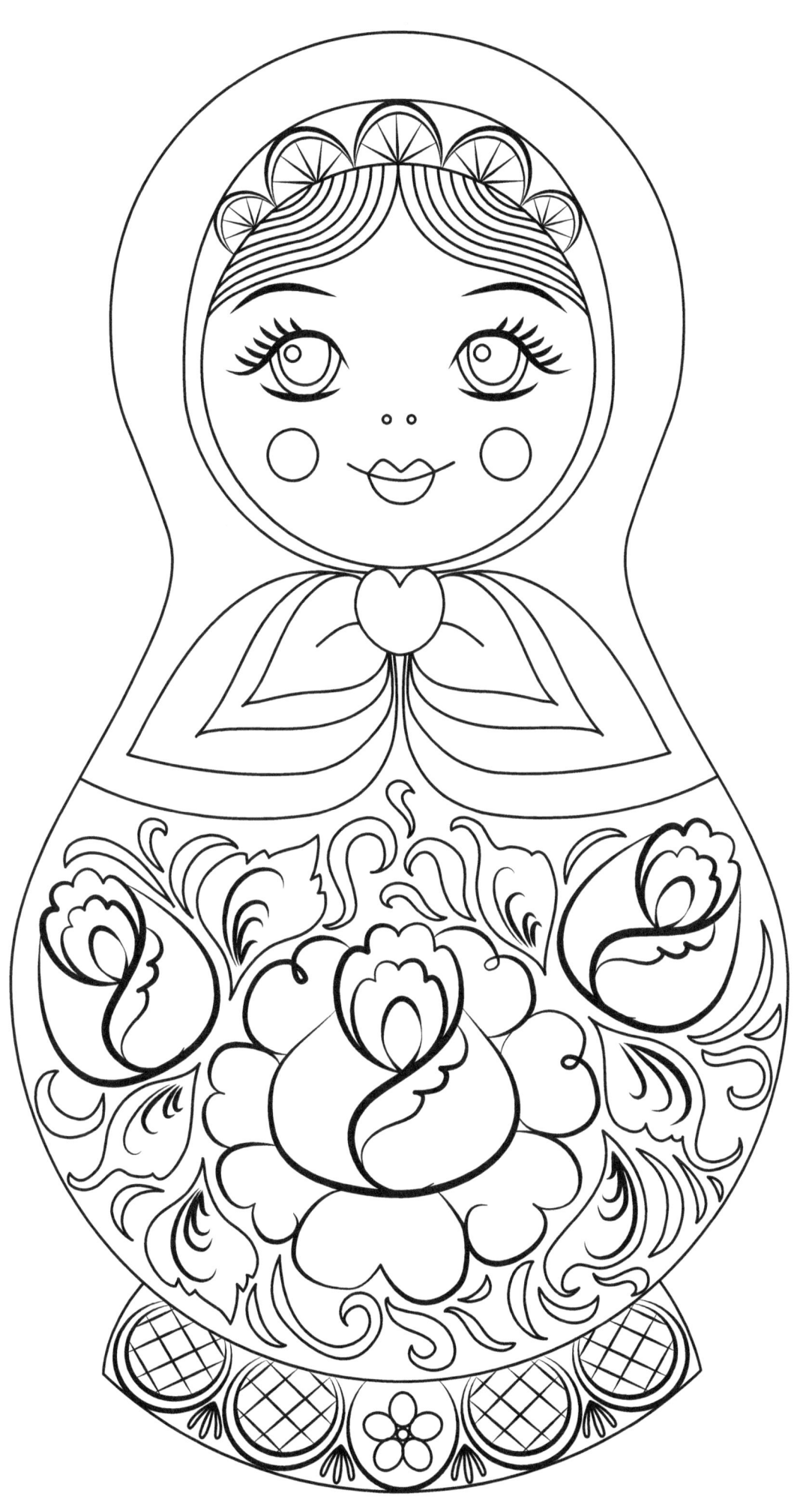

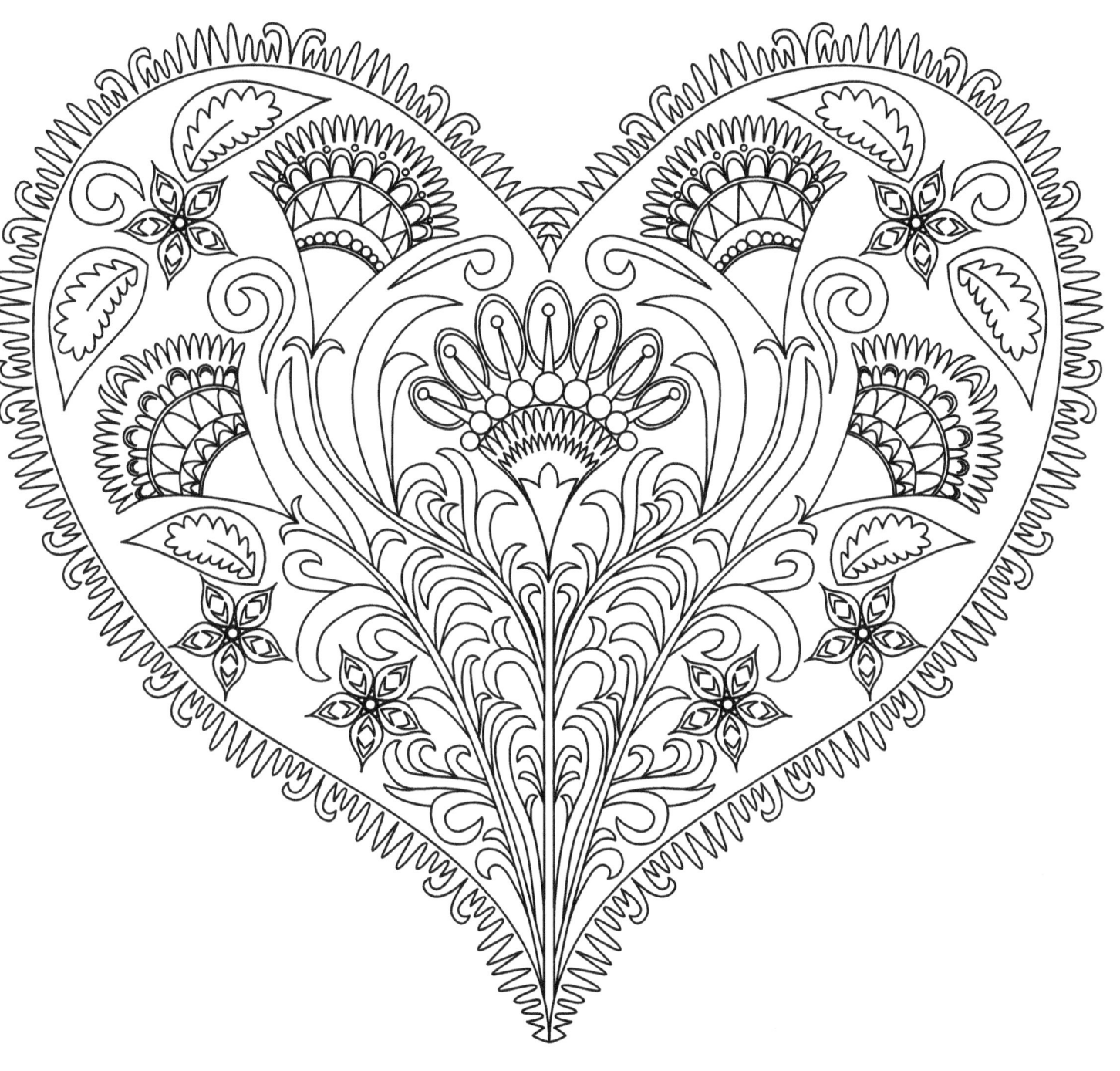

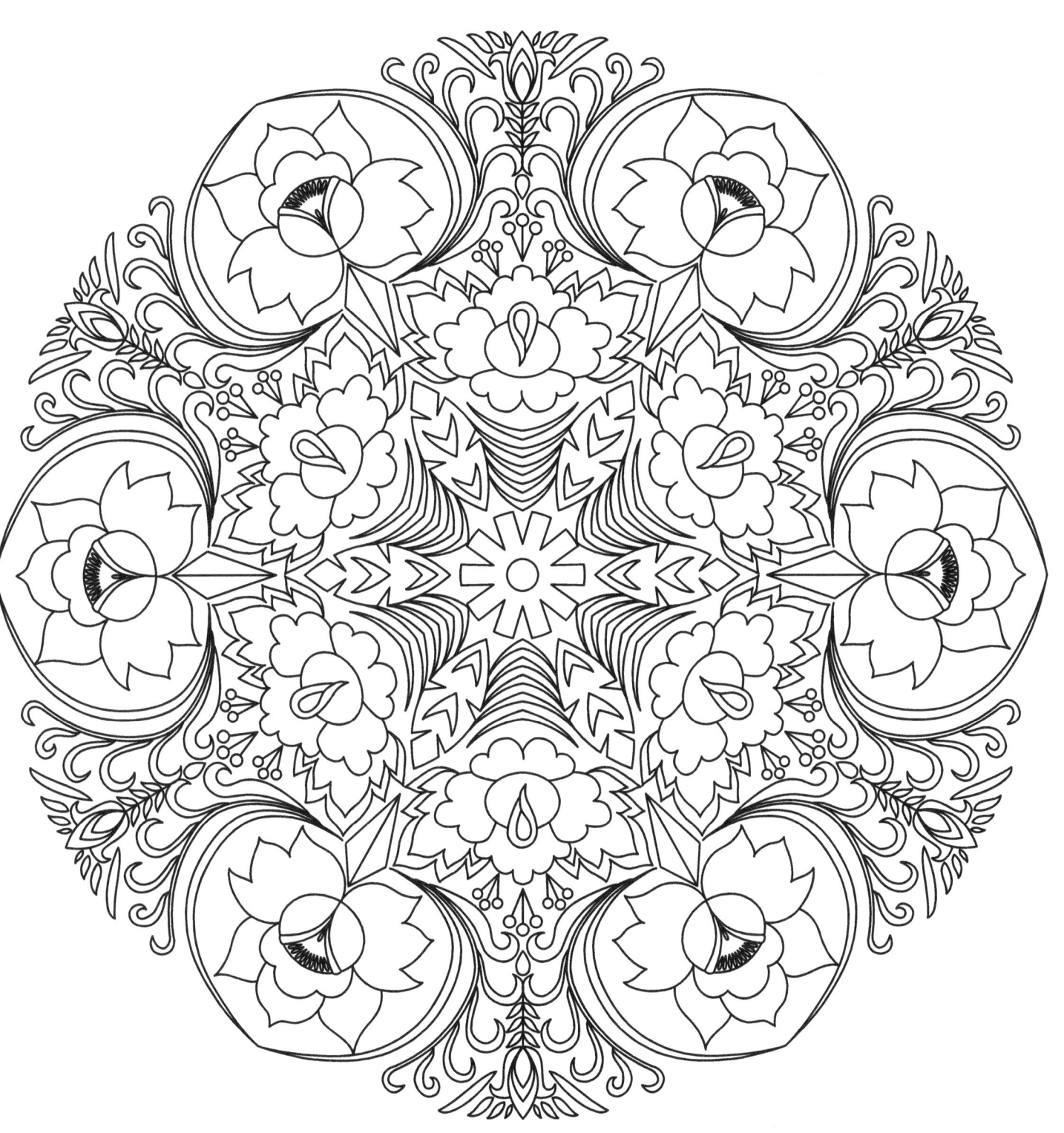

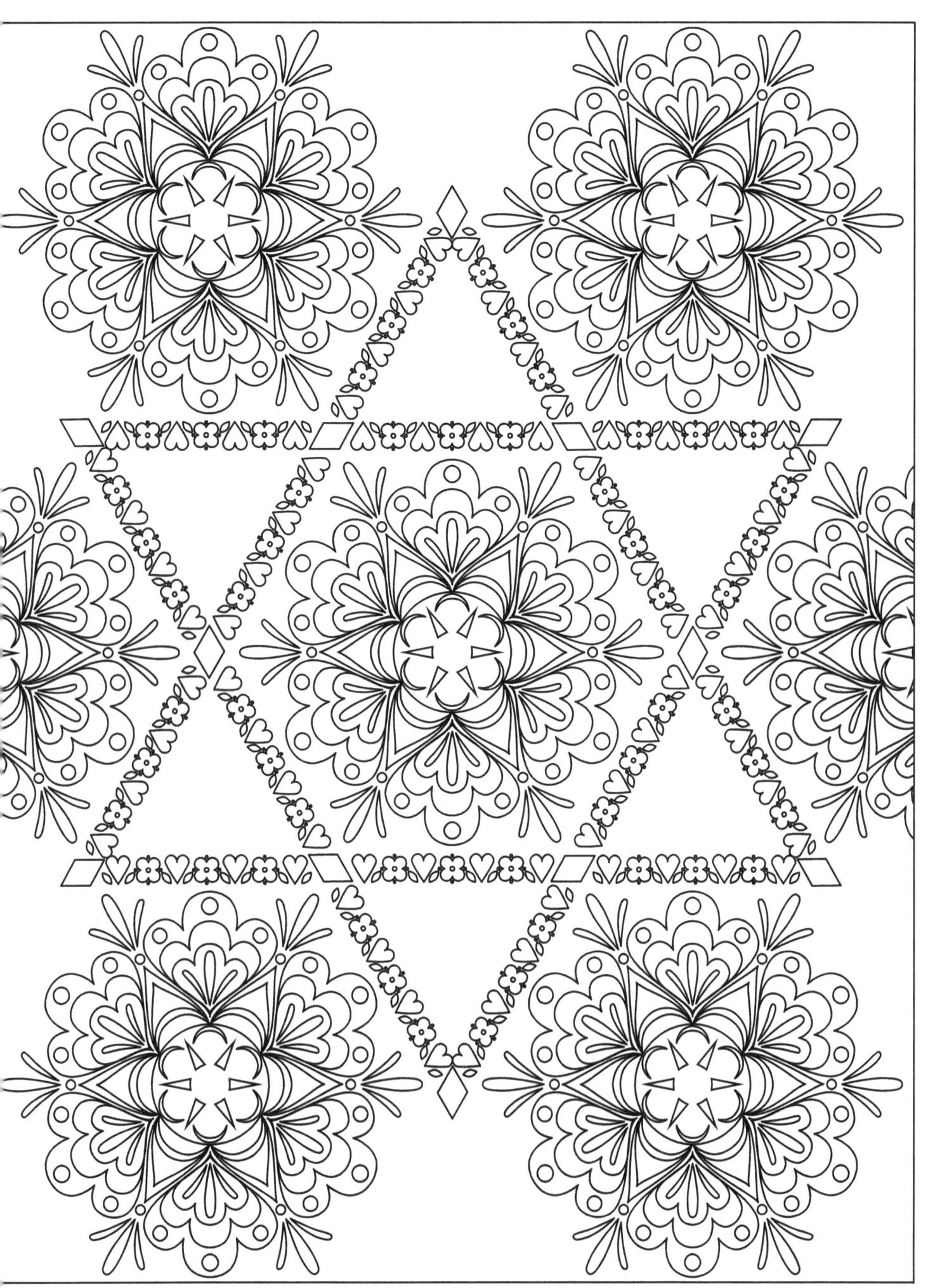

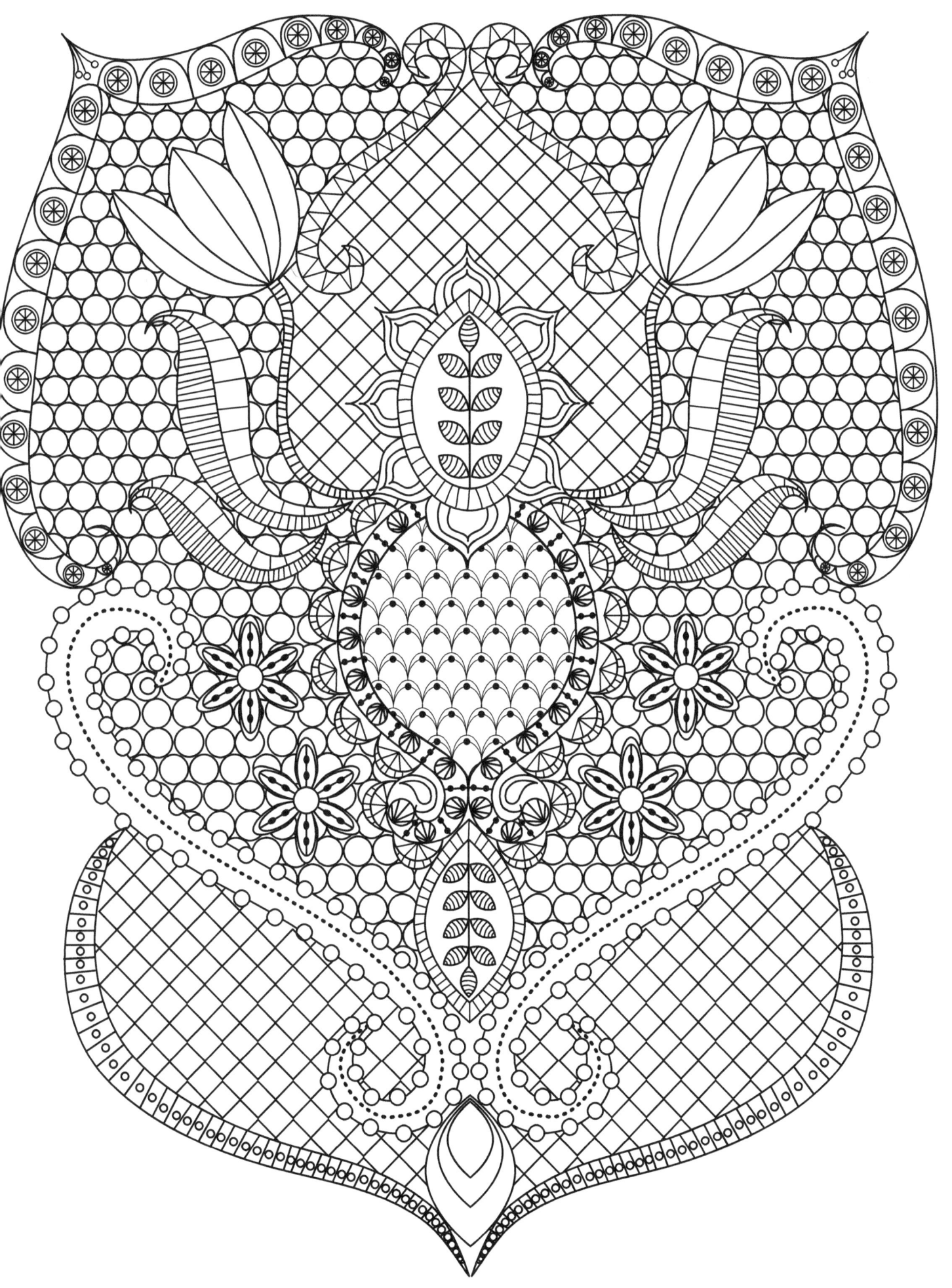

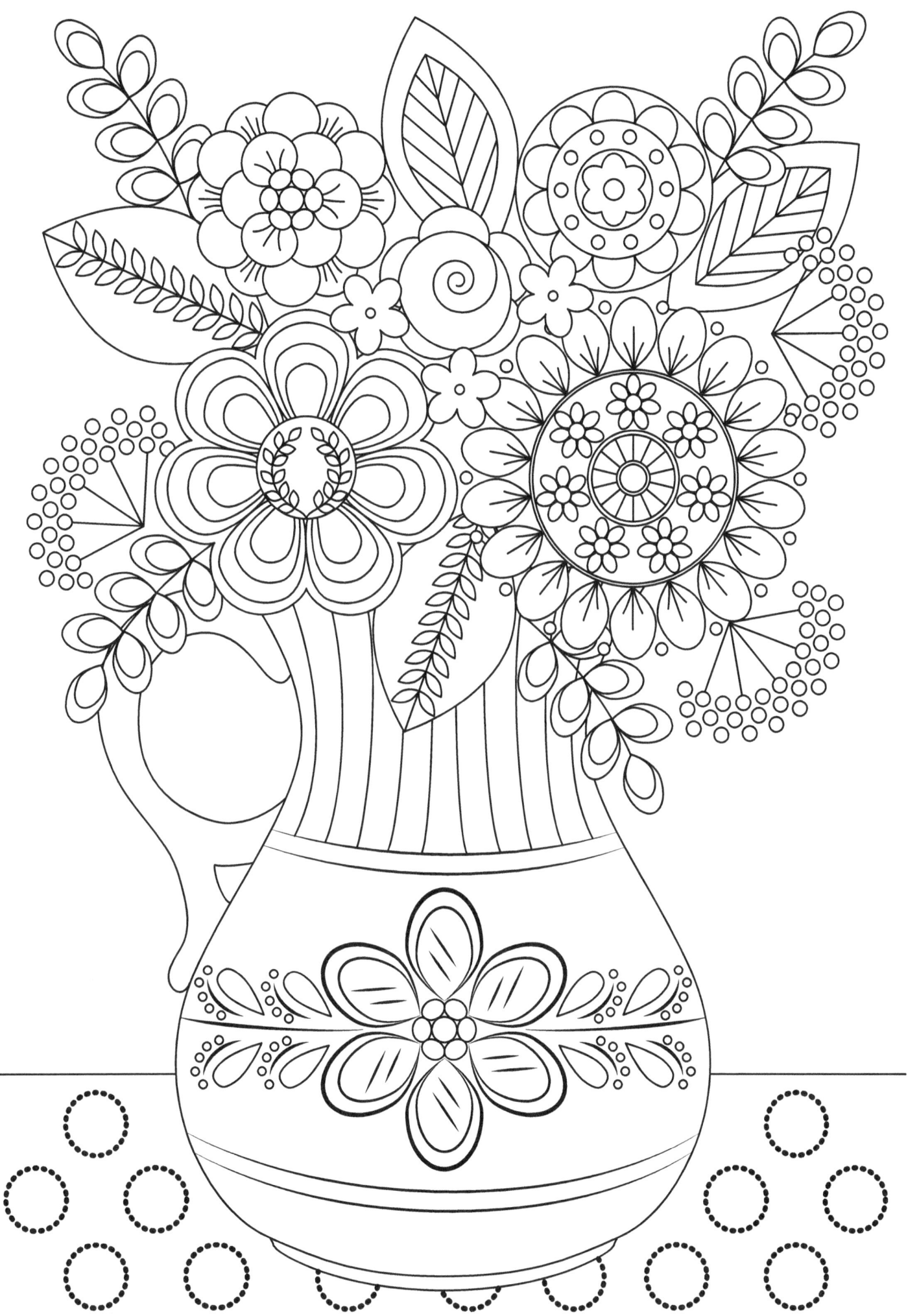

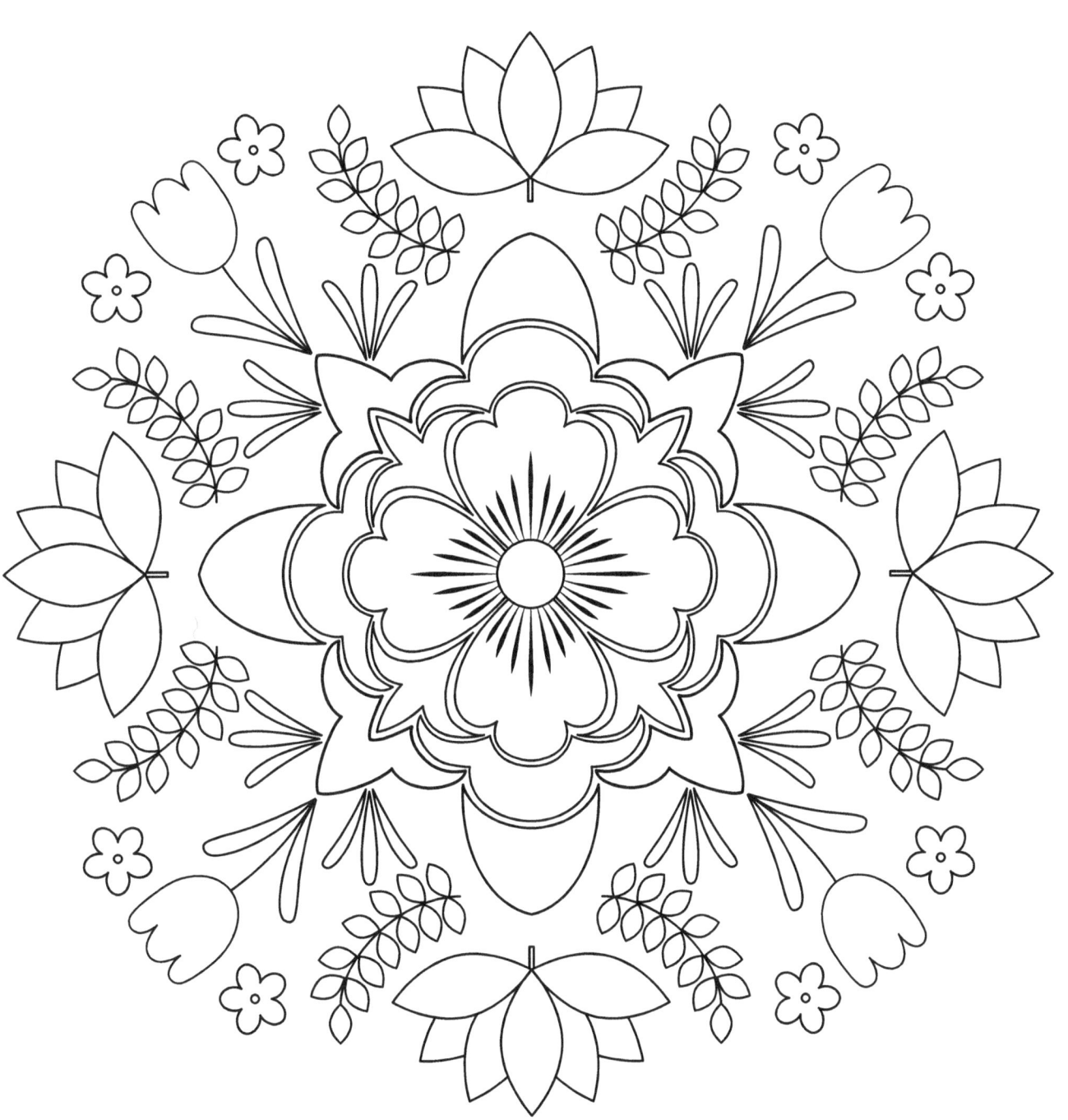

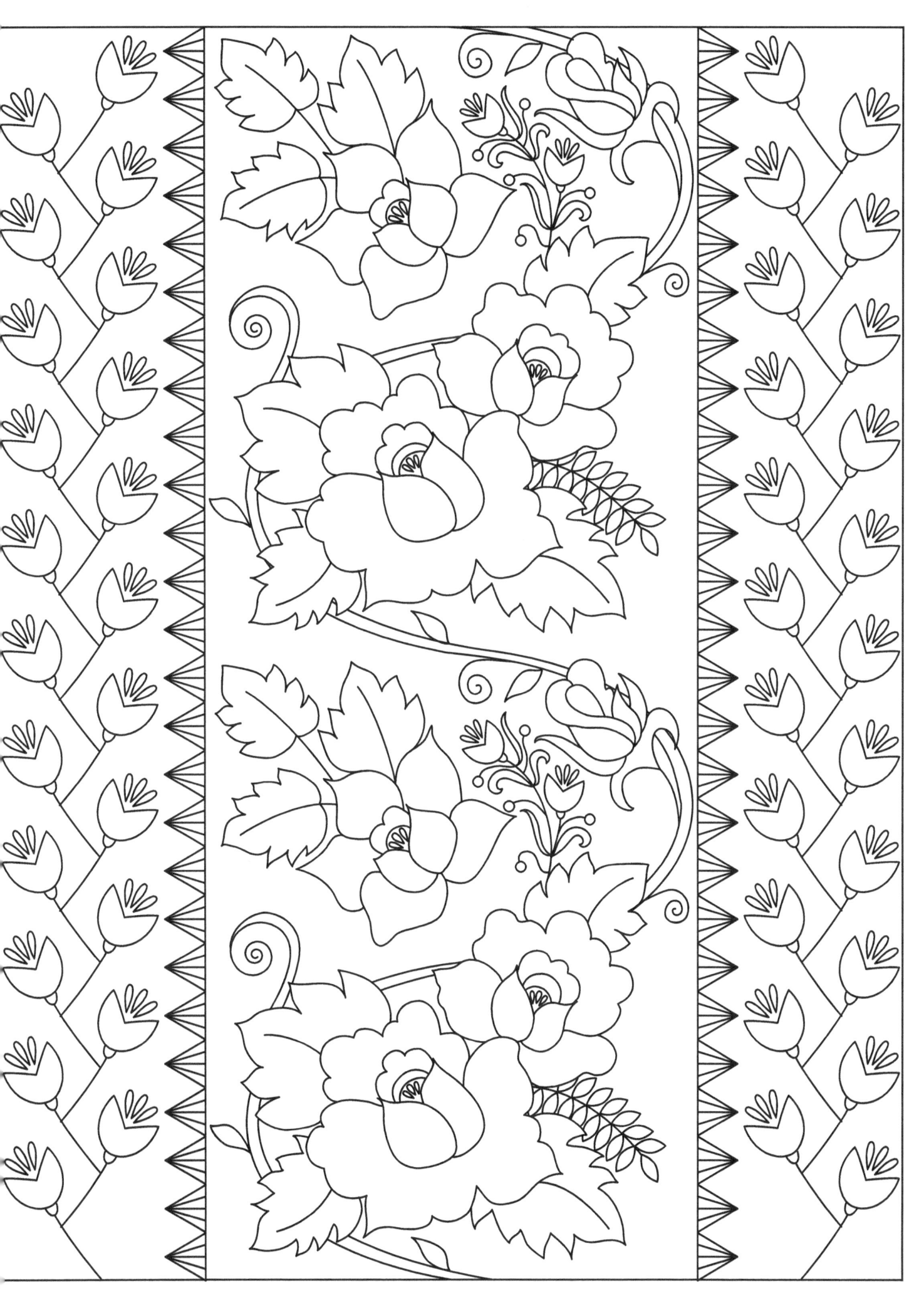

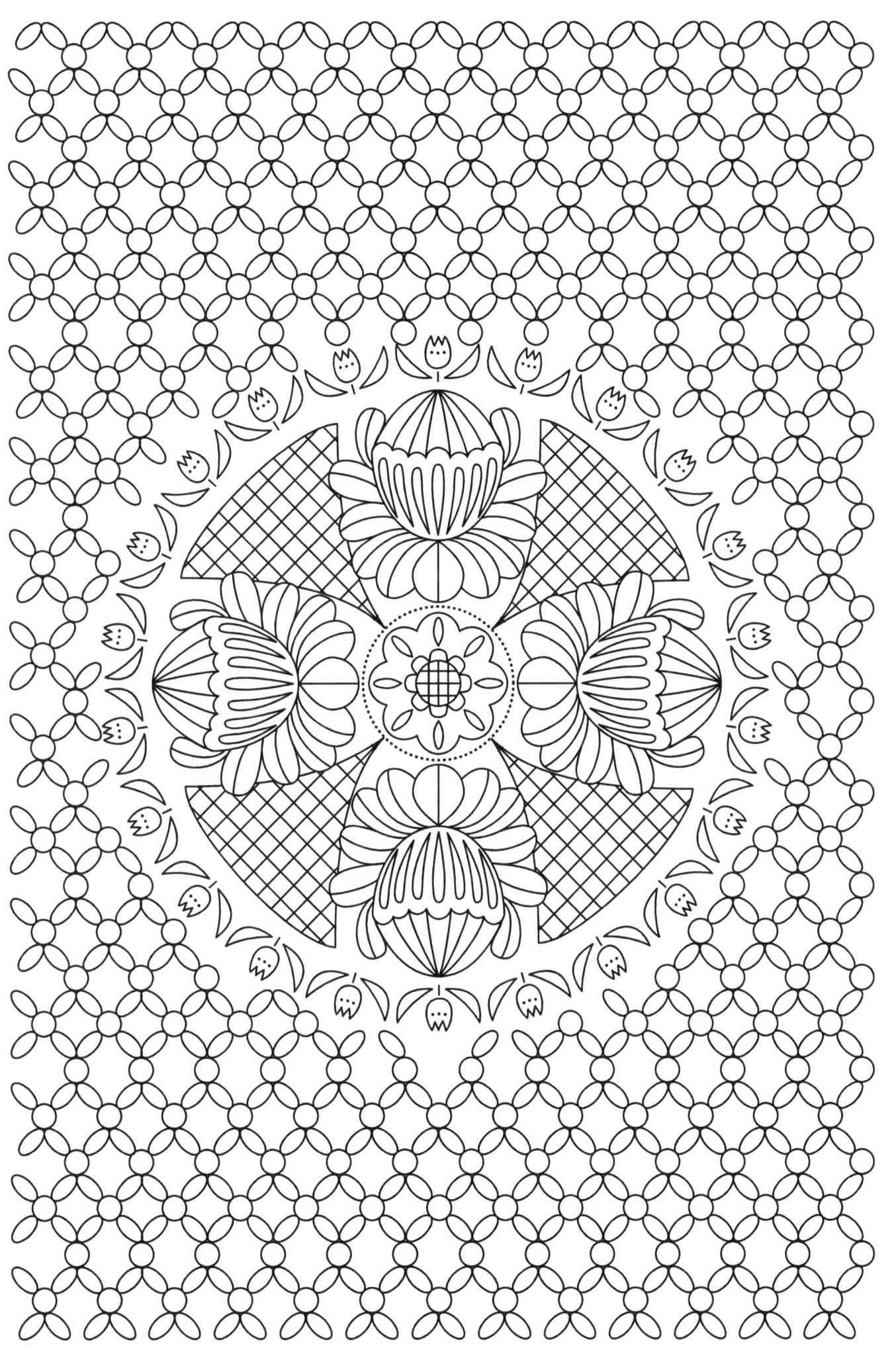

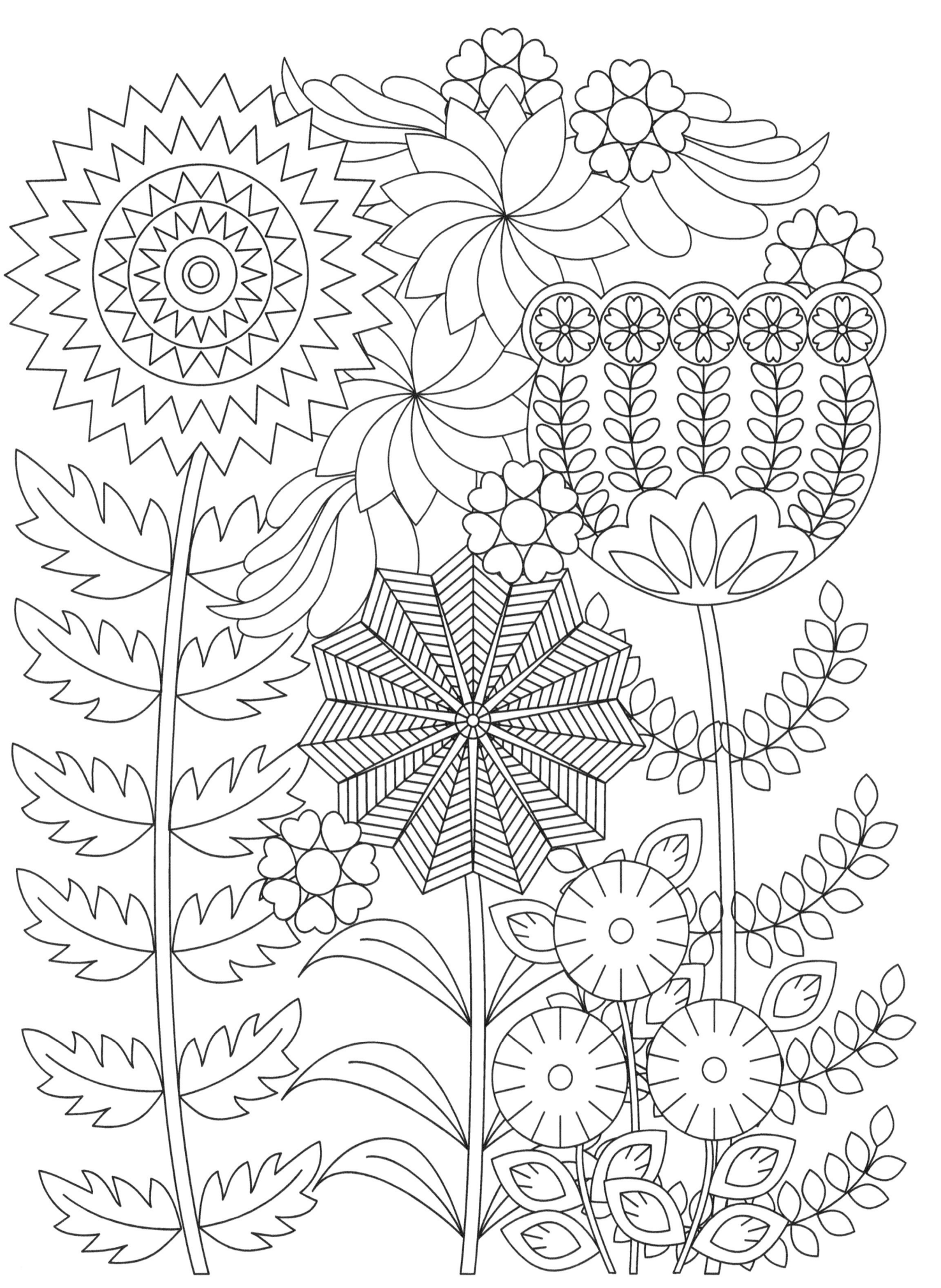

About the Artist

Anneline Sophia is a surface pattern designer and illustrator, working from her eponymous studio, based in the UK. Anneline grew up in South Africa, an experience that has influenced her work, especially her love of beautiful floral patterns, vibrant colors and nature-themed designs. She loves to travel and is inspired by folk art and folk embroidery work.

Her designs have been licensed by various companies around the world. Her designs are feminine and colorful, usually with hand-drawn or hand-painted elements that make her designs bold, eye-catching and beautiful.

The designs and patterns in this book are for personal use only.

Please feel free to share your colored pages from the book on social media and with Anneline by using the hashtag #AnnelineSophiaColor and tagging her.
www.facebook.com/AnnelineSophiaDesigns
www.instagram/AnnelineSophia
www.twitter.com/AnnelineSophia

Thank you for purchasing this book. If you have enjoyed it, please leave a review on Amazon. This helps to make the book more visible on Amazon so that more people can find and enjoy it.

If you are interested in licensing these or any other of Anneline's designs for use on your products, please contact her via her website or email:
www.annelinesophiadesigns.com
info@annelinesophiadesigns.com

Anneline Sophia